THE EXTRAORDINARY AMAZING INCREDIBLE UNBELIEVABLE WALLED CITY OF KOWLOON

by Fiona Hawthorne

BLACKSMITH BOOKS

The Extraordinary Amazing Incredible Unbelievable Walled City of Kowloon

ISBN 978-988-79639-3-6

Published by Blacksmith Books
Unit 26, 19/F, Block B, Wah Lok Industrial Centre,
37-41 Shan Mei Street, Fo Tan, Hong Kong
Tel: (+852) 2877 7899
www.blacksmithbooks.com

Also by Fiona Hawthorne:
Drawing on the Inside – Kowloon Walled City 1985

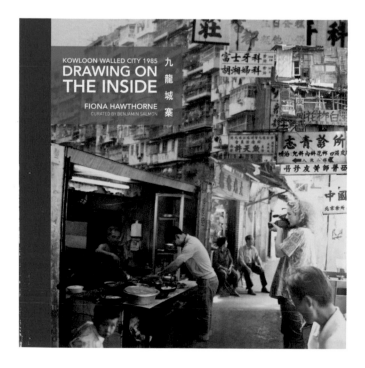

For my children
Sasha, Rudi, Eden and Benjamin
and for the children of the
Walled City of Kowloon

There was once an extraordinary place called the Walled City of Kowloon.

It was in Hong Kong, on the south coast of China, and there was nowhere else like it on Earth.

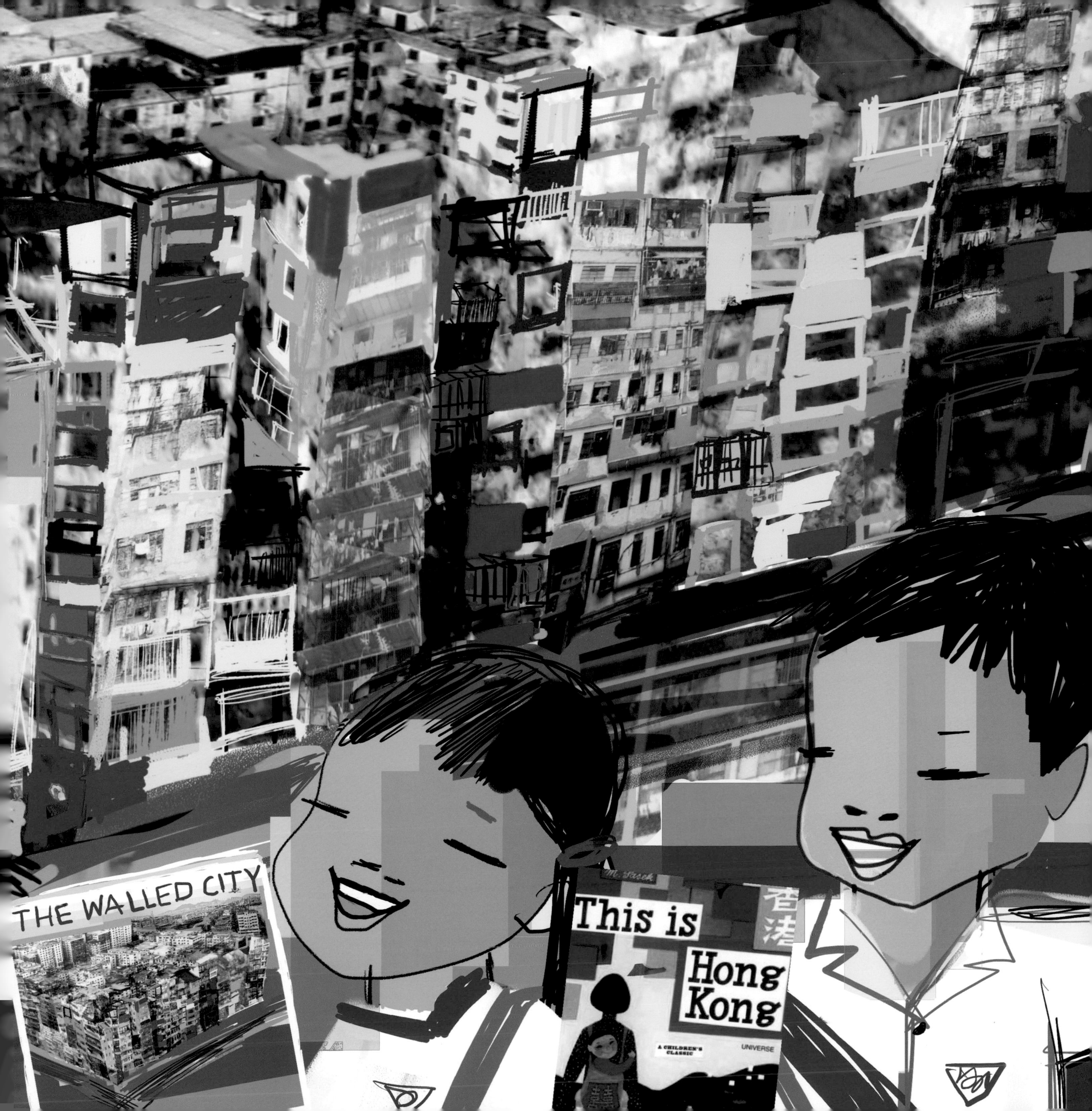
THE WALLED CITY
M. Sasek
This is
Hong
Kong
香港
A CHILDREN'S CLASSIC
UNIVERSE

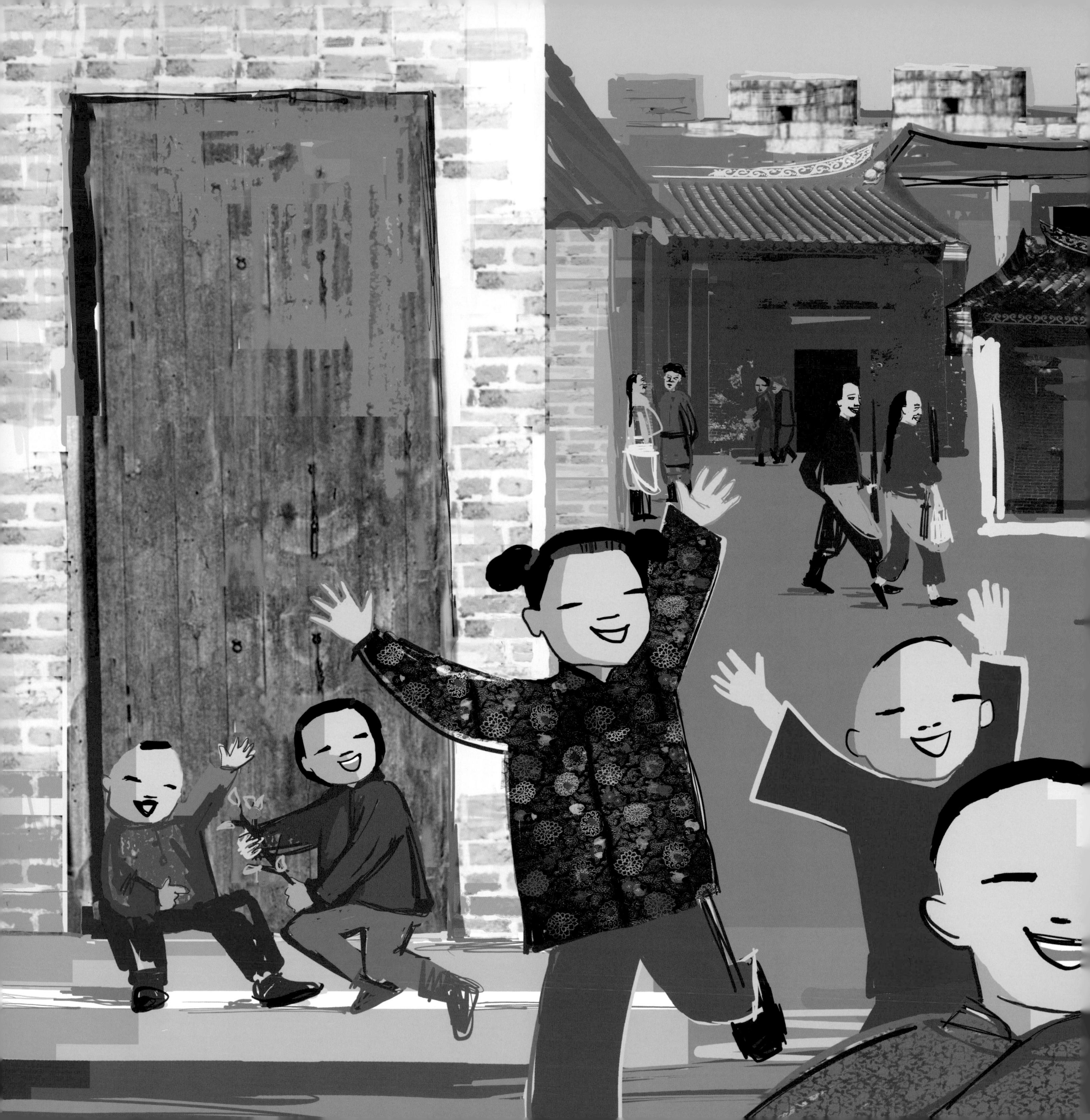

The Walled City began as a small, important Chinese fort surrounded by a strong stone wall. Inside the wall lived the leaders of the area, as well as an army of soldiers and their families.

As time went on, things changed outside the Walled City.

British sailors and merchants came and took control of Hong Kong Island and Kowloon. Then, they took the New Territories too, but only for 99 years. After the 99 years was over, the land would go back to China.

This meant that although the Walled City and all the rest of Hong Kong was in China, it was ruled by Britain. But because the Walled City was unique, and it was still surrounded by its own wall, many people believed it was still ruled by China.

At first the Walled City stayed the same, but when things changed in the rest of Hong Kong, the Walled City changed too. The leaders and the army left, many of the old buildings fell down, and eventually the Walled City was almost totally deserted.

Then everything changed!

Many new people came to live in Hong Kong. They came from all over China and they needed somewhere to live and work. Some came to live in the Walled City.

Landlords built new blocks – they said that people needed new homes. They said the Walled City was not like the rest of Hong Kong, that it still had its own rules and its own laws, so they built the new blocks very quickly. Later, people added extra floors to make the blocks even taller.

The buildings were packed together so tightly that every space was filled. Some buildings leaned on others, some had no power or tap water, and some were a mismatched patchwork of jumbled shapes.

The old wall was soon gone. The Walled City now had an invisible wall.

More and more people came to live in the Walled City and it soon
became the busiest, most densely populated place in the whole world.
It looked incredible and unbelievable!

Some people said the Walled City was not a real city. It was messy and jumbled and it spoiled Hong Kong, and it should be changed or demolished. Other people said it was special, unique and even beautiful. It should be left alone and allowed to work its own way.

Either way, the Walled City of Kowloon was part of Hong Kong's history, part of Hong Kong's skyline, and part of many people's lives.

Around the edges of the Walled City, where the old wall once stood, there was every kind of shop and business. People came to buy things or to visit the many doctors, or dentists who would fix their teeth for only small amounts of money.

Some people said the doctors and dentists were not legal and should be shut down. Others said it was lucky they were there – they helped the people of Hong Kong.

There were no roads in the Walled City of Kowloon, so people walked in and out through narrow gaps between buildings. The gaps led to dark alleys lined with dripping pipes and tangled cables that brought power and water into homes and factories.

Some people called the Walled City "The City of Darkness."

But other people said it was a wonderful place, full of colour and life and things to see, and when you went inside it was like stepping into an adventure…

Machines clacking, metal screeching, fans whirring, woks hissing, fish frying, knives chopping, people laughing, children running, music playing, water dripping… the people of the Walled City worked hard to make many things, from dumplings and dim sum to tools and toys.

All of the things were packed into boxes and taken outside, to sell in shops in the rest of Hong Kong.

And all over the world children noticed that some of their special toys had the words "Made in Hong Kong" stamped into the plastic.

But many of those special toys were really made in the Walled City of Kowloon.

Steep flights of stairs led up to the roof. The tops of the many blocks made a giant puzzle of spaces to jump to and explore, amongst a forest of TV aerials.

Some people thought it was dangerous on the roof, but the children of the Walled City loved to play there and look out over Hong Kong.

They watched planes land at nearby Kai Tak Airport, on the runway that stretched out into the sea. The runway was made from the strong stones that once formed the old wall around the Walled City. The old stones had been re-used when the wall came down.

The planes thundered overhead so low it felt like you could reach up and touch them. The sound from the engines was deafening and exhilarating!

One day, a girl called Fiona came to the Walled City with pens and brushes and paints. She returned day after day to work, and people made space and sat still so she could paint their portraits.

She never forgot the kindness of the people.
They stayed in her drawings forever.

People came to the Walled City to run schools or to help people who were sick. Fire inspectors came. They said that the jumbled pipes were not safe and that there could be an accident. They worried that if a fire happened it could spread quickly… it could be difficult for people to escape down the steep staircases and through the narrow alleys.

Photographers and film makers came. They worried that someday the Walled City would be gone. They wanted people to remember it like it was.

Many people thought the Walled City could not go on forever… something had to change. There were public meetings and it was decided that Kowloon Walled City had to go.

New homes were found for people to move to, and some people were happy to go. Other people wanted to stay… they loved their extraordinary and incredible Walled City.

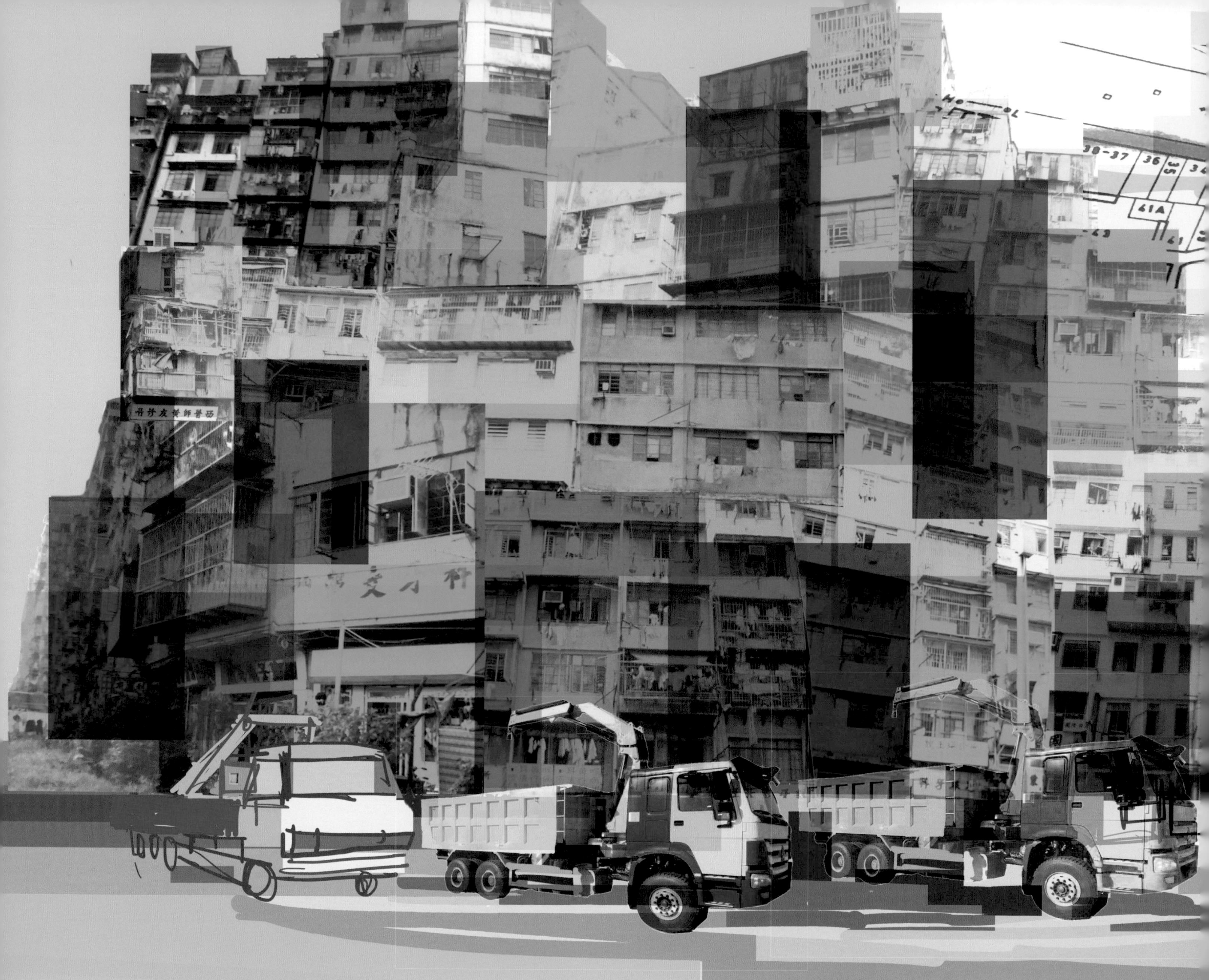

One day the demolition began.

Block by block, clump by clump, the Walled City was taken down.

Eventually the Walled City of Kowloon became an empty space, leaving only the shape of where the old wall had been.

Everyone watched and wondered what would happen in the space… would a new Walled City be built, modern and gleaming like other parts of Hong Kong?

But the people of the Walled City knew it could never be rebuilt. They wanted the space to become something new, something different, something very special…

Hong Kong listened and the wish came true.

And now, if you go to Hong Kong, you can still visit the Walled City of Kowloon.

You can learn all about its history because the story is told in a small museum, in the middle of a beautiful garden, where the Walled City once stood.

It is called "Kowloon Walled City Park" and it is unique and peaceful and very, very beautiful.

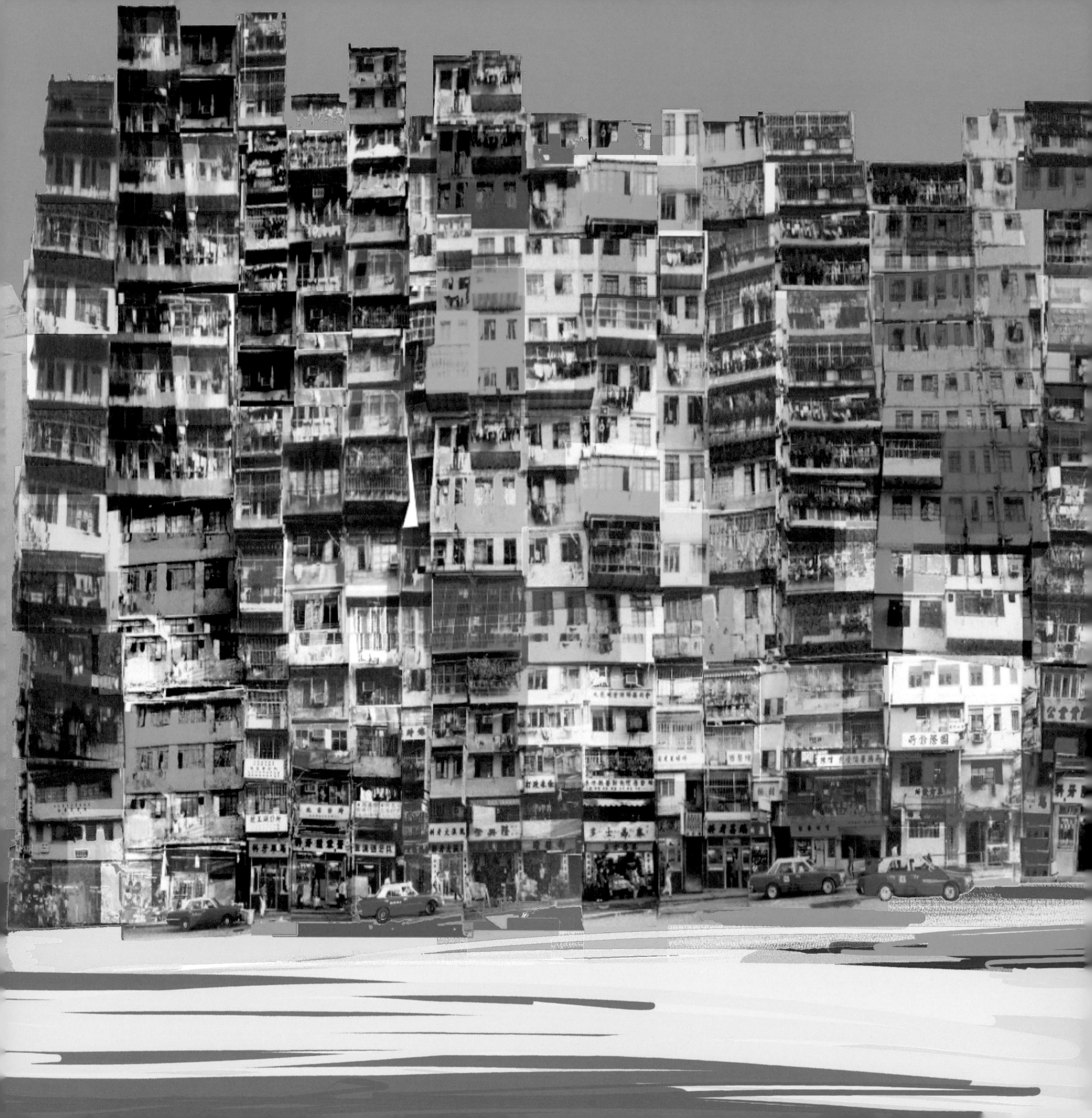

The Walled City of Kowloon was once one of the most amazing and extraordinary places on Earth...

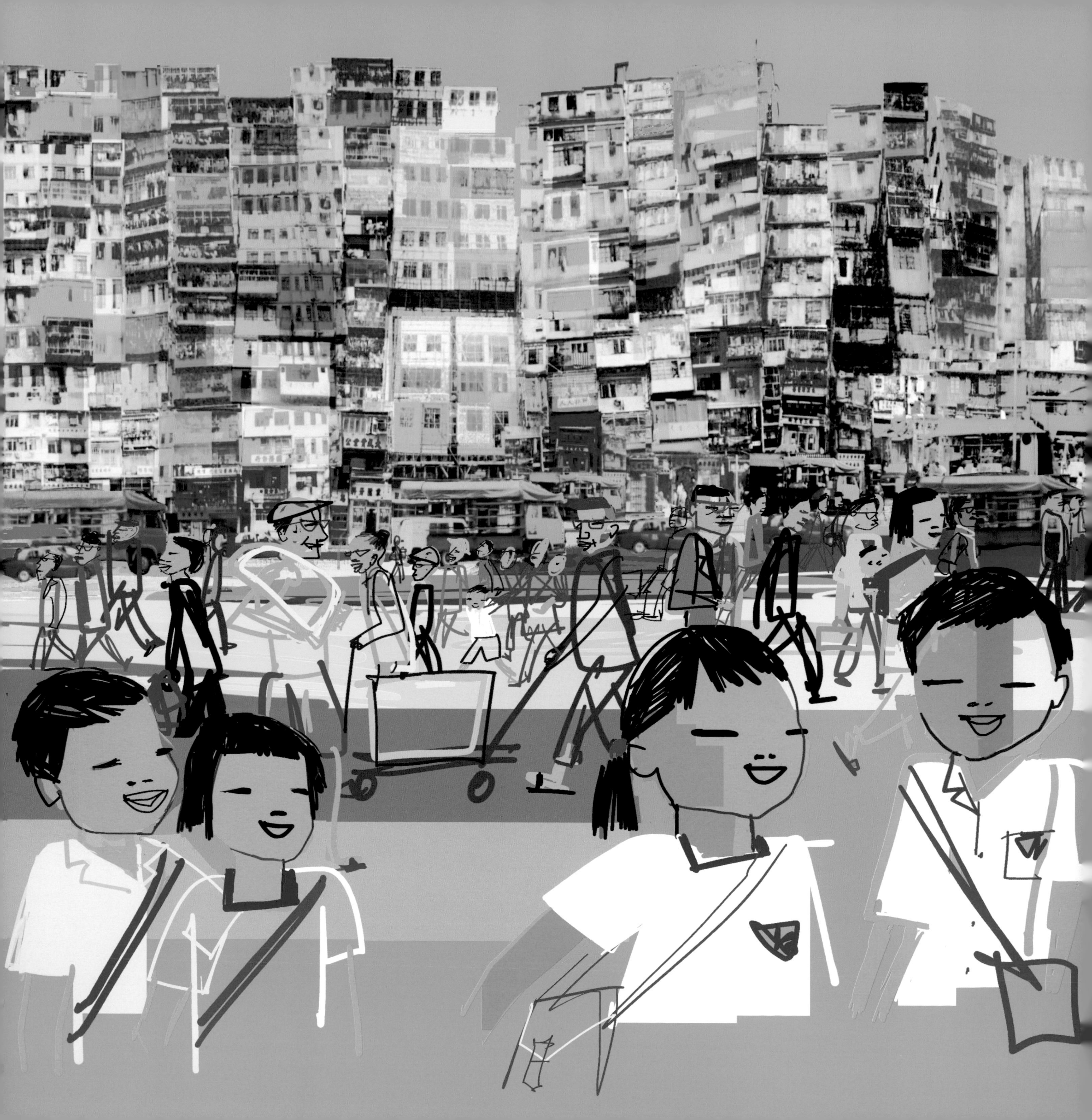

And many people who visit the park to remember the Walled City say that it still is.

The story Behind the Book
which can be read by adults (and also by children)

I was a child in Hong Kong in the 1970s. I loved everything about my home... the colour, the noise, the heat, the neon, the crowds and chatter, the smell of markets and street food and fresh fruit, the rainwater rushing down the gutters, the oily ferries in the busy harbour, the high-rises, the hillsides and forests and reservoirs, the shopping malls, the things you could look at – or sometimes buy – everywhere you went.

I drew the things around me all the time: the busy buildings and street scenes, the people and children. I had sketchbooks full of people with invented stories. I especially loved one street market near the old Kai Tak airport, full of clothes and toys, where aeroplanes roared overhead. It was right by an extraordinary place called the Walled City of Kowloon, but I had only seen that place from a distance. I had never been inside.

Seeing the Walled City close up for the first time was totally unbelievable and difficult to describe. Imagine looking across an already exciting skyline where old buildings meet new high-rise blocks. But suddenly, right before your eyes, the scene changes and something about the next 500 metres is different, odd, unbelievable. The Walled City of Kowloon looked shocking and unexpected. Still high-rise, but chaotic and disordered. Blocks seemed to have been joined together and added-to randomly, leaning against each other haphazardly, like a clump of building had seeded in the wrong place and grown accidentally into a different one! The Walled City of Kowloon was a patchwork of strange beauty.

Then, my family left Hong Kong. We went to live in the UK. I missed Hong Kong desperately. Some part of me had been left there. I still felt connected to the place that was my true home. I had to go back.

Luckily, six years later I returned to Hong Kong, and it was then that I went inside the Walled City of Kowloon for the very first time. A friend led me through one of the dark alleys with dripping pipes and jumbled cables and took me to meet people she knew there. Straight away, I knew I must get to know the Walled City. I had to draw and paint it.

Inside the Walled City, I found people to talk to and places to sit and draw, paint and film. I met only warm and kind

people. I didn't really have a plan, and I had no idea that I was recording a place that would one day be gone. I spent three months there. Then, my drawings and paintings were put away for 36 years while I finished my studies, met my husband, raised four children and worked as an artist in London.

But the Walled City artwork was stored carefully in my loft, and it was often on my mind. I felt I had to show the work and tell its story, but how would I do it?

Over the years, I heard other people talking about the Walled City, but they only said bad things: it was dark and crowded, the businesses did not have the proper licences, and outlaws hid there. This did not seem fair when I thought of the children I had met in the Walled City. What memories would those children – now adults – want to pass on to their own children? Would the colour, the adventure and the community spirit of the Walled City become lost, or could it still be shared?

So, 36 years after I went there, I created *The Extraordinary Amazing Unbelievable Incredible Walled City of Kowloon* to share the story with everyone!

A magical thing happened when I saw a photo posted in an old pictures group on Facebook. It was shared by Scott Siu-Fei Wong, and it was a photo of him as a boy on the roof of the Walled City. The roof was his playground when he lived there. Scott's photo was the first time I had seen a happy memory from someone else, and I felt so excited – my memories from long ago were real! I wrote to Scott, who now lives in Australia, and sent him my first draft of this book. Scott loved the book and sees it as a joy to share with his kids and other kids, and this means so much to me.

I have loved every minute of making this book. I have mixed history in with my personal adventure and memories that I truly cherish. I have thought hard about what is important to share and I hope you can see that the Walled City gave me not just colourful images to create from, but also welcomed me with kindness, acceptance, support and grace.

I hope that adults who remember the Walled City will enjoy sharing this story with their children, and that children who never knew it can get a picture of a wonderful, unforgettable place. The Walled City of Kowloon truly was like nowhere else on Earth.

Fiona Hawthorne

Siu-Fei Wong
28 January 2019

This is me in 1978. The place I lived is called the walled city in kowloon city. My family lived there from 1977 to 1981. My friends and I often played on the top of the building. Notice that there were no safety barriers anywhere. We did skateboarding, we played soccer & we jumped from building to building. It is pretty scary when you think of it but I didn't know any better. On right is the old airport. Planes flew over us just seconds before they touched the runway. They came so close, they were big and loud and it was truly breathtaking.

You, Steve Garcia, Pete Spurrier and 413 others   152 comments

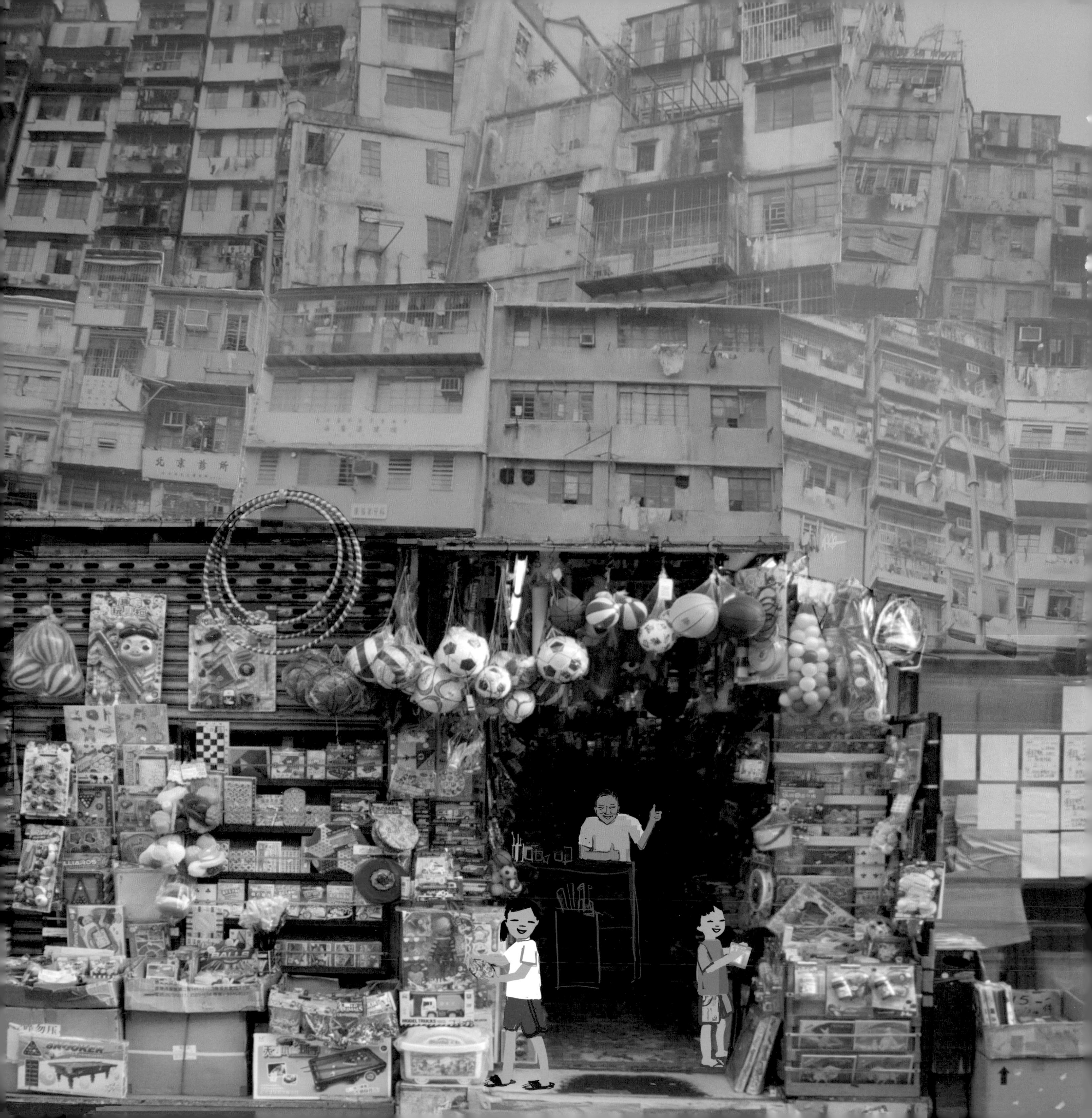
SNOOKER
MODEL TRUCKS